THE
BEAD
·BOOK·

THE
BEAD
·BOOK·

Juliet Bawden

PIATKUS

For Nigel, Carol and Steve

Copyright © Juliet Bawden, 1987

First published in 1987 by
Judy Piatkus (Publishers) Ltd, 5 Windmill St, London W1P 1HF
Reprinted 1988

British Library Cataloguing in Publication Data

Bawden, Juliet
 The bead book.
 1. Beadwork
 I. Title
 746.5   TT860

 ISBN 0–86188–564–3

Edited by Susan Fleming
Illustrated and designed by Paul Saunders
Photography by Helen Pask

Phototypeset in Linotron Baskerville by
Phoenix Photosetting, Chatham
Printed and bound in Great Britain at
The Bath Press, Avon

Contents

Working with Beads **6**
History of Beads **7**
Types of Bead **9**
Findings, Threads and Tools **13**
Beads from Found Objects **17**
Beads from Paper **20**
Beads from Clay **21**
Decorating Beads **23**
Bead Necklaces **26**
Bead Earrings **35**
Bead Hair Decoration **42**
Sewing with Beads **43**
Bead Weaving **45**
Acknowledgements **48**
Stockists **48**

Working with Beads

The *Shorter Oxford English Dictionary* defines 'bead' as 'A small perforated body, of glass, amber, metal, wood, etc., used as an ornament.' This gives us a starting point. But, when you think about it, a bead can be almost anything – and almost anything can be a bead. For some of the beads in this book are not made of such traditional materials. There are beads made from sweets, pasta and balloons; there are also beads of crystal, mother of pearl and blown glass.

This book offers a new craft which does not involve a large financial investment. Beads are generally inexpensive. They also take up very little room: you can do bead work from a tray on a hospital bed or on the corner of the kitchen table. There is no storage problem either, since tools and beads can be packed away in a biscuit tin or shoe box when you have finished.

Some ideas are purely for fun whilst others show you how to make a piece of jewellery to be treasured. Learn how to make earrings, necklaces, chokers; how to weave and sew with beads. There are also ideas to keep children amused on wet afternoons: for example, making beads from paper, clay or pasta.

Why not turn your new-found skills into a small business? Local clothes or gift shops might be interested in selling your wares. Try and get a stall in a local market or try a 'boot' sale and see how you get on. Once you have learnt how to put beads together, you will have attractive gifts of earrings and necklaces to give away as birthday or Christmas presents.

This book shows you some ways of putting beads together. Use it as a jumping-off point for your own ideas. Have fun!

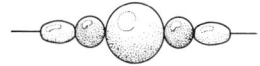

History of Beads

Jewellery, much of it in the form of beads, has been the answer to man's profound need for self-adornment, and is consequently one of the oldest forms of decorative art. We have evidence of the existence of beads going back 7,000 years to the early civilisations of Mesopotamia (Iraq) and Egypt.

Beads have also been worn for purposes other than adornment. They were, and still are, often worn to show the status and wealth of the wearer. In medieval Europe, including England, laws and decrees proclaimed that only certain classes of society could wear certain categories of jewellery. In many cultures beads and other forms of jewellery have been worn for amuletic (protective) purposes. In China, jade (nephrite) was believed to hold magical qualities, and was thought to help the dead to ascend to heaven and escape the terrors of the underworld.

As the Egyptians were buried in their everyday jewellery, it has been difficult for historians to distinguish between funerary, amuletic and secular jewellery. The materials they used, as well as the forms they carved them into, had significance. For example red carnelian was the colour of life blood, green felspar or turquoise meant new life, and blue lapis-lazuli was the colour of the heavens. Falcon or bull amulets gave the owner powers by assimilation. Other amulets represented something to be avoided – such as the scorpion. Many of the amulets had holes carved in them so they could be worn as beads.

In many African cultures even today beads are worn to signify age or status of the wearer. In her book *Africa Adorned*, Angela Fisher gives many examples of this. She tells how most of the nomadic tribes of east Africa are ordered into an age-set system, their body adornment providing an outward sign of their age and status. 'Maasai women wear flat neck collars made of beads and spaced with strips of cow hide. Nborro (long blue beads) are worn only by married women, as are the beaded snuff containers worn round their necks. The Maasai say that blue beads are "god", as they are the colour of the sky he inhabits, and green beads are "vegetation after rainfall", the symbol of peace.'

Married Toposa women are distinguished by their hairstyle of tiny pigtails finished with red seed beads. 'Tight beaded corsets are everyday wear for some of the Dinka men, the colour indicating their position in the age-set system: red and black are worn by 15–25 year olds; pink and purple by the 25–30 age set, and yellow by those over 30.' 'Alluring bead bodices are worn by Dinka girls who are eligible for marriage. . . . Beads, provided by the girl's family, are applied in patterns which indicate the family's prosperity, and cowrie shells are attached to promote fertility.'

Man's recognition of the intrinsic quality of certain materials – such as precious metals, and gems – has led to their constant use in totally unconnected cultures separated by both time and distance. Gold, being one of the most precious and coveted metals, appears in the form of beads in many cultures. Interestingly enough, according to Angela Fisher, the people of the Sahara prefer to wear silver – 'the pure metal blessed by the prophet' – rather than gold – 'the metal of the devil' – which is feared and believed to bring bad luck.

Beads are among the commonest objects found during excavations at prehistoric sites in Western Asia. The demand for exotic materials out of which beads could be made is thought to be a significant factor in the growth of trade networks in prehistoric times. The invention of glazed faience, a forerunner of glass, made it possible to imitate scarce varieties of coloured stone at relatively low expense. From *Africa Adorned* again: 'Glass beads, originally brought from Persia and China by Arab traders, and later from Europe by the Portuguese, were widely used as a form of barter. By the turn of the century, mass-produced beads from Europe were being traded by the million along the East African coast. These were known as "trade-wind beads" in Kenya, and as "pound beads" (sold by the pound) in Sudan.'

As you will find, when you read the next chapter, we are still using the materials used by early civilisations.

Try and visit museums such as the Victoria and Albert or the British Museum and look at beads. You will find that the same images, forms and shapes recur throughout the different ages and cultures. And you may be surprised at how very modern some ancient Sumerian and Egyptian jewellery looks.

Types of Bead

Beads come in all shapes and sizes and are made from many different materials. Here are just some of them. All the beads mentioned below are available from the stockists' list on page 48. Both Ells and Farrier and The Bead Shop sell catalogues giving the colour, dimension and price of the beads.

Glass

Plain
These are usually round or tubular in shape with a smooth surface.

Faceted
With many cut sides, these come in various shapes – for example, round, oval and teardrop.

Shapes
Some of these beads include glass or wire loops from which the bead can be hung. Shapes include roses, leaves, cherries, aubergines, bananas, oranges, strawberries, corn on the cob, grapes, carrots, miniature dolls, shrimps and dolphins.

With Silver Paper
These beads come in many colours, the silver paper in the middle giving them a lustrous appearance.

African Trading Beads
Brightly coloured and patterned, they were used originally to buy slaves.

Crystal
High-quality cut glass, clear in colour, producing wonderful rainbow effects when hit by light. Usually round or a 'drop' shape.

Marble
These beads look like children's marbles made of clear glass containing dribbles of colour.

Rocailles
These are tiny beads and have many uses. They are used in bead weaving by the North American Indians. They were the basis of the beaded purses and dresses worn by the 1920s flappers; and they come in opaque colours, transparent, silver-lined, iridescent, pearlised, striped or with a metallic finish. You can even buy them with off-centre holes.

Bugles
These are long slender beads, often used for sewing onto garments or hair combs.

Wooden

Unpainted Soft Wood
These beads are round and range in size from 15mm (¾ inch) to 50mm (2 inches) and are particularly easy for children to thread. They are ideal for painting.

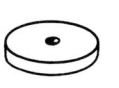  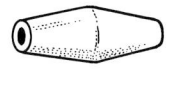

Painted Soft Wood
Soft wood beads come in many shapes including washers or flat discs, round, semi-spherical, oval, square, tubular.

Red Wood
This is a close-grained Canadian wood. Although the wood has some red in it, the beads are a combination of warm colours ranging from cream and pale yellow to a warm rusty red.

Palm Wood
In the form of washers, round, or oval beads, they are cream with brown lines.

Coconut
Beads of a round shape or round or irregularly shaped washers. They are naturally cream coloured but may be dyed. They are sometimes treated with wax to give a better finish, but this can make them greasy.

Cinnabar
A vermilion coloured wood used in China and Japan. Usually hand carved with tight geometric patterns.

Ebony
A hard black wood sometimes carved, sometimes inlaid with metal. The beads come in many shapes such as washers, cubes and round.

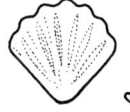     

Shell

Mother of Pearl
Mother of pearl can come in its natural colour or be dyed turquoise, pink, red, orange, yellow, brown or green. The most common mother-of-pearl bead shapes are round, tulip or rice. It also comes in the following forms: star, love birds, heart, seagull, leaves, cross, eagle, mushroom, fish, shell, elephant, crescent moon, dolphin, seahorse,

teddy bear. Sometimes these shapes are pierced with a hole or they hang from a 'bail' (see page 13).

Baroque or Fresh Water Pearls
Baroque pearls are nubbly, creamy white in colour and a fraction of the price of cultured pearls.

Apple Coral
Red-brown in colour, often with black veins running through it.

Sea Urchin
Looking like shell or ceramic, these are actually the spines of the sea urchin and make beautiful dangly earrings.

Plastic

Plastic beads come in many forms, colours and finishes including metallic ones. Some do not look as good as other beads but many have as good a finish as the beads they are emulating. They are light, often inexpensive and do not break as easily as, for example, glass beads.

Metal

When one thinks of metal jewellery it is the precious metals such as gold, silver or platinum which spring to mind. However base metals such as copper and brass are used a great deal for making beads. Sometimes these are plated in silver or gold.

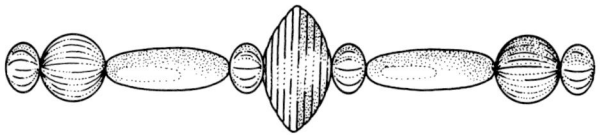

Findings, Threads and Tools

Findings

A 'finding' is the metal mount to which a piece of jewellery is attached. There are findings for earrings, brooches, bracelets, necklaces, etc. They come in such a variety of metals and styles, that I have mentioned below only the ones most commonly used.

Findings for Earrings

For pierced ears you will need a stud or a hook (for example, a kidney wire), both of which are pieces of wire that go through the hole in the ear. Some studs and hooks come with a disc on which to stick beads, others have loops from which to hang them.

For pierced ears, it is advisable to use silver- or gold-plated findings to prevent infection.

Earring findings for unpierced ears are either screw-on or clip-on; they too have either loops for hanging or discs for sticking.

Head Pins and Eye Pins
Beads are usually threaded onto head pins or eye pins. These are pre-cut pieces of wire, and come in various lengths. Head pins look like dressmakers' pins without a pointed end. Beads rest on the 'head'. Eye pins have a loop or eye at one end for suspending beads.

Bead Cup
Bead cups sit on the end of head pins, like miniature saucers, and are used to prevent beads with large holes from falling off.

Bail
If you wish to suspend a cone- or drop-shaped bead you use a bail; this is a piece of wire bent into the shape of a triangle.

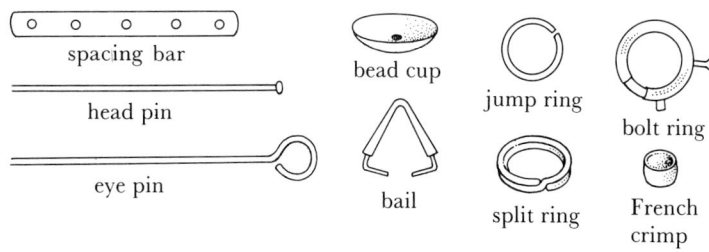

Jump Ring
Jump rings are split rings that come in various sizes and are used to connect one piece of jewellery to another. For example you can hang two or three eye pins or head pins from one jump ring and then hang the jump ring from the earclip or wire.

Spacer Bar
A spacer bar is a pretty, decorative piece of metal with a loop at either end, used as an alternative to pins, for hanging beads.

Findings for Necklaces

Many of the findings used for earring-making are also used for necklace-making: jump rings and eye pins, for example, can be used in drop necklaces.

Spacing Bars
If you are making a choker or just wish to keep the strands separate use spacing bars. These are bars with holes at regular intervals through which to pass the thread.

Split Rings and Bolt Rings
These are used to fasten a necklace. Split rings look like miniature key rings and are used at one end of a necklace with a bolt ring at the other.

French Crimp (Crimping Bead)
If you are using a thread such as 'Tiger Tail', a very strong nylon-coated steel thread, you will not be able to tie knots in its end so you will have to use a crimping bead (French crimp), in the following fashion.
1. Thread the beads onto the 'Tiger Tail' (TT for short).
2. Thread the crimping bead onto the end of the TT.
3. Thread the end of the TT through the loop on the bolt ring or through the jump ring when finishing the other end of the necklace.
4. Take the end of the TT through the crimping bead, and pull tight so that the beads are close to the crimping bead.
5. Squeeze the crimping bead tightly with a pair of flat-nosed pliers: this will hold the TT firmly thus stopping it from moving.
6. Cut off any excess TT.

Box Clasp
If you are making a multi-stranded necklace you will need a box clasp fastening.

Other Fastenings
There are various types of screw clasp which may also be used to fasten necklaces, as well as hook and eye fastenings.

You will soon discover the kind that is most suitable for your purpose.

Threads and Wires

Copper and silver wire are the most commonly used in jewellery-making and they come in many thicknesses. The thickness is commonly known as the SWG or Standard Wire Gauge, or dimensions are given in millimetres. 4mm (about ⅛ inch) and 6mm (about ¼ inch) were are most commonly used in earring-making. The 6mm holds its shape better than the 4mm and is suitable for making jump rings or bails.

When choosing thread consider the following: Is the thread going to show? Is it strong enough for the beads? Is it the correct thickness for the holes in the beads?

Nylon gut is ideal for children to use as it is easy to thread without a needle.

Tiger Tail, described on page 15, is ideal for heavy beads. It too can be used without a needle.

Fine brass wire or nylon thread is ideal for fine beads such as rocailles. Again it is not necessary to use a needle.

Waxed terylene is a very strong, all-purpose thread which is easy to use without a needle and comes in various thicknesses.

Laces made from rubber are great for fun or junk jewellery and are available from Hobby Horse (see stockists, page 48).

Leather thongs are good for making ethnic jewellery and for beads with large holes.

If you are wishing to knot between beads for a decorative effect use silk or thick cotton.

You could also use shearing elastic – even lighting flex or cable!

Tools

You do not need many tools for putting beads together. There are three which are particularly useful. The first two are available from Hobby Horse.

1. A pair of round-nosed jewellers' pliers. These are used for twisting wire into different shapes and for making loops at the end of pins. They are round in section.

2. A pair of flat-nosed jewellers' pliers. These are used to squeeze the ends of wire together, for example when closing a jump ring. They are D-shaped in section.

3. A pair of tin snips for cutting wire. These are available from hardware or DIY shops.

If you are using bugle beads or rocailles it is useful to have a beading needle. This is a very long, fine sewing needle. It is essential to have one of these for bead weaving.

Beads from Found Objects

'Beads' can be made from almost anything! Although they may not be strictly definable as beads, they are used in the same decorative ways, and some of the following ideas will amuse you!

Look also at natural sources, such as shells, bits of driftwood, feathers, bamboo, pieces of bone, animal teeth, seeds or even small pebbles with holes. With the exception of the pebbles, all of these may be turned into beads by drilling with a hand drill using the finest drill bit you can find. Your local hardware store will sell drill bits. Thread any of your 'found' beads onto raffia, leather thonging or shoelaces to create an ethnic look.

Edible Beads

Edible beads are fun to make and children love them. Make a necklace or bracelet by threading sweets onto shirring elastic. The most obvious choice of sweets for necklaces are the mints with the hole in the middle. Various manufacturers produce a series of miniature sweets including 'candy tots' and 'jelly tots'. These, and the miniature liquorice allsorts, look equally good as necklaces or earrings (see photographs).

Miniature Sweet Necklace

1 packet of sweets, as above
enough shirring elastic to thread to make a necklace fit over the head
1 blunt needle (an embroidery needle is ideal)

1. Thread the shirring elastic through the needle.
2. Push the needle through the sweets and thread them onto the elastic. The needle is likely to become very sticky – wipe it occasionally with a damp cloth.
3. If you want to keep sweet beads rather than eat them, give them a coat or two of polyurethane or clear nail varnish.

The Stationery Department

Find more 'beads' in good stationery departments in the form of brightly coloured plastic or metal paperclips which you can just link together (see necklaces photograph). Clip miniature bulldog clips, or plastic pegs approximately 3cm (1½ inches) long onto a cord or line to make a fun necklace.

Balloons

Balloon Necklace

1 packet of balloons
1 piece of black 2 core lighting cable 40cm (15¾ inches) long
1 eye pin
1 earring hook

1. Using a pair of dressmakers' scissors, cut the necks off the round balloons.
2. Cut the necks into 5mm (¼ inch) strips (so they look like miniature arm bands).
3. Cut the long balloons in the same way – you can use all but the round end.
4. Thread these pieces onto the cable. If they are loose, twist them into a double or treble loop before threading them, so that they fit.
5. Split one of the remaining balloon bodies so that you have two flat circles, by cutting along the fold line.
6. Pierce a hole in the centre of each circle with a pin.
7. Push the eye pin through the hole until only the loop is showing, holding the stalk of the eye pin alongside one end of the cable. Cover the end of the cable with the balloon circle. Roll up the last piece of balloon neck so that it holds both the eye pin and balloon circle in place.

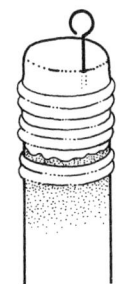

8. Repeat step 7 using the hook, for the other end of the cable. (See the necklaces photograph.)

DESIGN VARIATIONS
1. Use white cable.
2. Thread with coloured elastic bands.
3. Use flex (such as for an iron or an electric fire).

Balloon Earring

You can use this principle, too, to make a necklace: simply tie the strips of balloon onto flex, and intersperse with cut elastic bands etc. to lend colour and texture.

The quantities below are for one earring only – for a pair, double the quantities.

earring clip or wire
4 balloons, either 2 green and 2 yellow
  or 2 pink and 2 orange
  or 2 blue and 2 green
1 head pin
1 bead cup
2 or 3 small beads (optional)

1. Using scissors or pinking shears, cut down the length of the balloons making strips approximately 5mm (¼ inch) wide.
2. Thread the bead cup onto the pin head.
3. Using a pin or a pair of scissors, make a small hole in the centre of each piece of balloon and thread onto the head pin.
4. Thread on about twenty pieces, then thread on the beads if you are using them.

5. *Either* curl the remaining section of the pin head around some round nose pliers and pull so it looks rather like a spring; *or* bend the remaining section of head pin 5mm (¼ inch) in one direction, and then 5mm (¼ inch) in the opposite direction so that a zig-zag shape is formed.
6. Make a loop in the end of the head pin and thread on the earring clip or wire.

The Kitchen Cupboard

Pasta comes in the form of stars, letters of the alphabet, hearts and bows. It also comes as tubes of varying sizes, some ridged, others semi-circular or twisted.

These are all ideal for children to turn into beads. Make sure the pasta you choose has a hole for threading. Paint the pasta with non-toxic water-based paints. When the pieces are dry, thread them on to shirring elastic. If you wish to protect your pasta necklace give it a coat of clear nail varnish.

Toys

Make a necklace by threading together brightly coloured wooden beads interspersed with small toys from Christmas crackers or miniature dolls-house toys and models. Thread these onto a piece of plastic, rubber or leather thonging.

You can buy plastic and rubber creepy crawlies, skeletons, bats, snakes and dinosaurs in toy shops. As the rubber tends to be very thin they can be pierced easily with a pin and threaded singly or as a gruesome collection onto jump rings and earring clips to make earrings.

Beads from Paper

This is one of the easiest and cheapest ways of making beads. Use old birthday cards, magazines, wrapping paper or even newspaper to achieve different looks. You can use plain paper and paint the beads before varnishing (see page 25).

Paper Beads

paper
a knitting needle or pencil
glue (a glue stick is ideal)
clear nail varnish
a lump of plasticine

1. Draw triangles, the same size as the pattern opposite, onto your paper (although the size of the beads can be varied according to the size of the triangle used).
2. Cut out a triangle and roll it round the knitting needle or pencil from the broad end to the pointed end.
3. Glue the pointed end into the centre of the bead you have just rolled.
4. Take each bead off the needle and leave the glue to dry whilst you make the next bead.
5. When you have made a number of beads thread them back onto the knitting needle.
6. Stand the sharp end of the knitting needle in the plasticine whilst you paint the beads with the clear nail varnish.
7. When dry, thread them together to make a necklace – nylon gut is best.

Beads from Clay

The clay used for making the ceramic beads in this book is known as cold clay. It is a product which has been developed by The Fulham Pottery Ltd of London and is available by mail order (see list of stockists, page 48). It is a self-hardening modelling material which does not need to be fired. It takes two days to harden at normal room temperature (65°F/18°C) but is firm enough to handle and decorate in half a day.

It can be decorated with the following: poster paints, acrylic colours, spray paints, enamels, ordinary household paints. It is a good idea to finish with a coat of varnish to protect the bead.

Clay Beads

cold clay or any self-hardening clay
a board on which to roll out
rolling pin
raw spaghetti or cocktail sticks
a lump of plasticine
paints for decoration
thread or leather thongs and other findings

1. *Long Beads.* Using your hands, roll on the board a long piece of clay about 5mm–1cm (¼–½ inch) in diameter, depending on the size of bead required, so that it looks like a snake. Cut into lengths of equal size and make holes through each piece with a piece of spaghetti, an eye pin, or cocktail stick. If you need larger holes use a knitting needle.

2. *Round Beads.* Make as for long beads, but once they are cut take each piece of clay and roll it in your hands to make a ball. Make holes as above.

3. *Square, Rectangular or Triangular Beads.* Make a long roll, as above, then flatten with a piece of wood, palette knife or a ruler, into a block that is square in section. Cut into oblongs or cubes, or cut diagonally to make triangles. Make holes as above.

4. *Coin or Medallion-Shaped Beads.* Make as for round beads and flatten with a rolling pin. Make holes in the centre for small beads and near the top for pendants.

Any of the above beads can have patterns or textures pressed into them to make them more interesting. Use coins, or anything with an embossed surface, to mark the clay.

5. *Flowers.* Make balls of clay about 1cm (½ inch) in diameter. Press the blunt end of a pencil

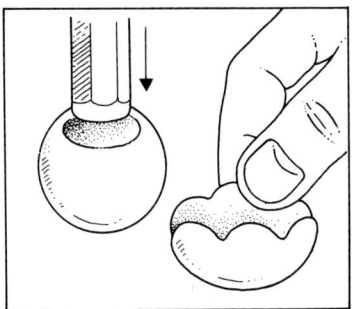

into the centre of the ball to make a bell shape. Squeeze the edges between the thumb and forefinger to give a frilled edge. Finish by making a hole in the flower centre.

6. *Leaves.* Cut elongated diamond shapes from clay. Frill the edges slightly (as for flowers), then make a hole in the top of the leaf.

Other Ideas

Look in children's books for inspiration. Look at simple stylised animals such as teddy bears, snakes, fruit etc. Keep the shapes fairly simple and add details such as faces, markings and clothes by painting them on afterwards (see page 25).

Decorating Beads

What to Decorate

Wooden beads, pasta beads, clay or ceramic beads can all be painted. Paper beads may be painted as paper before they are made into beads or as finished beads. You can decorate them with stripes, dots, wavy lines, or you can marble the paper first.

  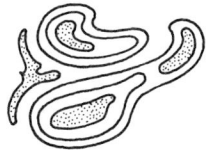

To Marble Paper

Mix a few blobs of oil paint with a few drops of white spirit. Fill a washing-up bowl with water and drip the paint/white spirit mixture onto the water – it will float on the surface. Stir the paint around to make swirly patterns. Gently lay the paper on top of the water and then carefully lift it off again. When the paper is completely dry, make into paper beads.

THE BEAD BOOK

Materials

Beads can be painted with almost anything, but see the various bead sections for further suggestions. Poster paints are ideal as they are opaque and dry quickly. As they have a chalky finish when dry, finish by coating with clear varnish after the paint has dried. Inks have a translucent quality. Wood stain does too: use this on wooden beads if you wish the grain to show.

Small tins of brighly coloured enamel paints may be obtained from toy, model and craft shops. These take a long time to dry but give strong colours and a shiny finish.

Permanent markers are an easy way of applying detail to beads.

1 Hanging Earring var. 5 p. 37; **2** Coin Earring p. 42; **3** Stud Earring p. 41; **4** Hanging Earring var. 5 p. 37; **5** Stud Earring p. 42; **6** and **7** Hanging Earring var. 5 p. 37; **8** Curtain Ring Hoop p. 39; **9** Stud Earring p. 42; **10** Hanging Earring var. 5 p. 37; **11** Red Oblong Diamenté Earring p. 42; **12** Hanging Earring var. 1 p. 36; **13** Hanging Earring var. 4 p. 37; **14** Hanging Earring var. 5 p. 37; **15** Basic Hanging Earring p. 36; **16** Hoop Earring 1 p. 39; **17** Hanging Earring var. 4 p. 37; **18** Hanging Earring using sweets pp. 17 and 36; **19** Flower Earring 3 p. 39; **20** Hanging Earring var. 2 p. 36; **21** Basic Hanging Earring p. 36; **22** Hanging Earring var. 3 p. 37; **23** and **24** Hanging Earring var. 5 p. 37.

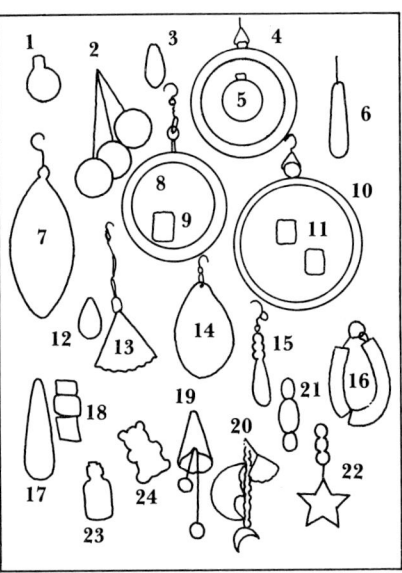

Facing page 25   Examples of old beadwork.

To Paint Beads

Before starting, collect together as many pencils as there are beads. These are to balance the beads on whilst painting. Also have a couple of jam jars, or pots in which to stand the pencils.

Wedge a bead onto the pointed end of a pencil so that it does not move. (If it doesn't fit, either sharpen the pencil or fit it onto one of another size.) You are now able to coat the entire bead in paint without having to touch it: just hold the pencil and turn it as you paint.

Leave each finished bead on a pencil standing in a jar until it is dry. Leave the bead to dry between coats.

If the bead is to have many colours and patterns, paint the first colour on to every bead before starting on the next colour.

If you are going to paint patterns try to keep them to the scale of the bead. Very simple motifs can be effective when used as an overall pattern. For example the white and green necklace in the centre photo-

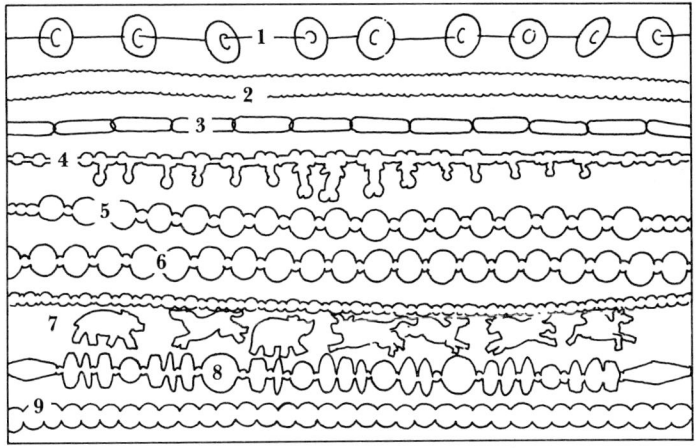

1 Edible Bead Necklace p. 17; **2** Balloon Necklace p. 18; **3** Paperclip Necklace p. 17; **4** Fruit Necklace p. 32; **5** Marble Necklace p. 32; **6** White and Green Necklace p. 25; **7** Animal and Bead Necklace p. 29; **8** Mixed Bead Necklace p. 29; **9** Yellow and Black Necklace p. 28.

graph consists of small white beads painted with tiny green triangles, alternated with smaller green beads.

When painting flowers look at forget-me-not, daisy, violet, primrose and other small flowers.

If you are painting a necklace of large wooden beads use bold colours and perhaps a striking abstract design.

Bead Necklaces

Before beginning to make necklaces – or bracelets, for it's the same principle – it is important to choose the right kind of thread and fastening for the beads you are using (see pages 13–16).

To calculate the number of beads required for a necklace work out approximately how many beads fit into 1cm or 1 inch (depending on whether you're used to imperial or metric), and multiply by the length required. As a rough guide:

- A short necklace is 40–50cm (16–20 inches) long.
- A medium necklace is 65–70cm (26–28 inches) long.
- A long necklace is 90–125cm (36–50 inches) long.

If you are short of beads, why not try one of the following:

- Knot between beads thus spacing them out.
- Use the interesting beads at the front of the necklace and smaller or less interesting beads at the back.
- Alternate the interesting beads with those of a smaller or less significant design.

Necklace Design

The necklaces in this chapter are guidelines to start you off in necklace design. I feel that the choice of beads and putting them together is a matter of personal taste and not something to be dictated.

Look in museums for inspiration. Go round the shops and adapt what you see to suit you. Look at jewellery worn in paintings, on the stage, in films, books and at what other people wear.

Before stringing a necklace, place different beads next to one another. Do the beads look good all the same size? Do they look better interspersed with smaller beads? Do you want to have a large bead as a centrepiece? Try contrasting colours, textures, sizes and materials (for example, wood and metal).

Helpful Hints

1. If you are making a necklace with a large central bead, put a needle on both ends of your thread in order to work from the middle outwards.
2. When making a necklace with pieces hanging from it, they will hang better if attached to jump rings.
3. Work a choker from the centre outwards, as the fit will be crucial. You may then add or subtract pieces from both ends.

Daisy Chain Bracelet

nylon thread
1 beading needle
16 bugle beads (blue or green)
48 white rocaille beads
8 yellow rocaille beads
1 bolt ring and 1 jump ring

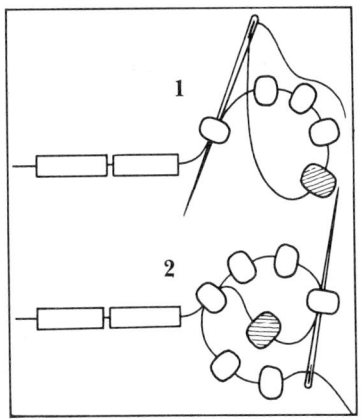

1. Thread the needle and make a knot approximately 10cm (4 inches) from one end to prevent the beads falling off.
2. Thread on 2 bugle beads, 4 white rocaille beads and 1 yellow rocaille bead.
3. Thread the needle back through the first white rocaille bead (fig 1).

4. Thread on 2 more white rocaille beads and take the needle back through the fourth rocaille bead (fig 2).

—27—

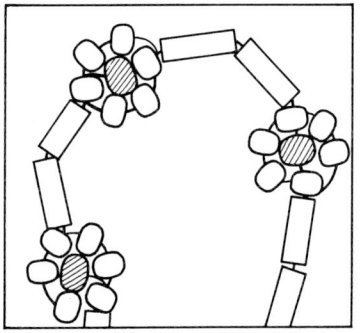

5. Repeat until all the beads are finished.
6. Attach the bolt ring to one end of the bracelet, the jump ring to the other.

Necklaces from Wooden Beads

The first two necklaces described in this section are made from painted soft wood. All have been threaded onto 'cotton perle', which is a thick embroidery thread. You could also, instead of the alternating effect, make wooden bead necklaces with half the length one colour, half another: I've had good effects with wooden washers in blue and red, and beads in pink and soft green.

1 Yellow and Black Necklace

(*see photograph between pages 24–25*)
This necklace is make by stringing together 50 black semi-spherical, and 50 yellow semi-spherical beads to form complete spheres made up of both colours. To add further interest, the order of threading black and yellow is changed so that in places there are 2 yellow beads back to back and in others 2 black beads.

2 Yellow and Black Caterpiller Necklace

In this, 67 × 4mm yellow beads are alternated with the same number of black wooden washers, thus giving the appearance of a caterpiller.

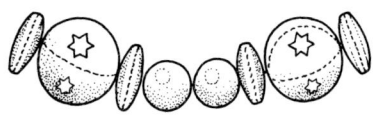

3 Inlaid Ebony Necklace

Made from 12 flat beads, 9 double beads and 8 beads inlaid

with stars. The beads for this necklace come from The Bead Shop in Neal Street (see stockists, page 48). The double beads and the flat beads are lighter than the beads inlaid with stars. The contrast of the bright wire against the dark coloured wood makes a very attractive necklace.

4 Ebony and Yellow Necklace
This necklace is made from a combination of painted orange/yellow beads and washers interspersed with heavier and more expensive carved ebony beads (available from Hobby Horse). The beads are threaded onto leather thonging and finished with a spring clasp (which looks like a spring with a loop at the end). The leather is pushed up the centre of the spring and then the spring is squeezed shut onto the leather thus holding it in place. The loop on one end of the necklace is opened up to make a 'hook', the one on the other end becomes the 'eye'.

5 Mixed Bead Necklace
(*see photograph between pages 24–25*)
This necklace is made up of many contrasting materials, colours, textures and shapes which when put together make a pleasing necklace. I used round red wooden beads, shell washers, palm wood washers and small metallic gold beads.

6 Animal and Bead Necklace
(*see photograph between pages 24–25*)
The beads – wood alternating with small gold beads – for this necklace come from The Bead Shop. The small carved animals have a hole down their centres. In order that the animals can be hung from the necklace, a head pin is threaded from the underside of each animal to its top. A loop for hanging is then made with a pair of round-nosed pliers at the top of the head pin.

7 Pink and Black Wooden Bead Necklace

9 black tubular wooden beads
15 dark pink tubular wooden beads
15 pale pink tubular wooden beads
11 dark pink oblong wooden beads
4 black oblong wooden beads
Tiger Tail
8 French crimps
1 fastening (jump and bolt ring)
eye pins
head pins
bead cups
7 jump rings

To make the main body of the necklace front.

1. Thread 8 dark pink oblong beads each onto its own eye pin and make a loop at the unlooped end of the pin. (The bead has to fit onto the pin without wire showing, other than the loops, at either end. If the pin is too long, trim off some of the wire.)

2. Connect 2 loops together with a jump ring. Repeat until 8

oblong beads are joined together with jump rings.

To make the hanging pieces.

3. Thread the remaining pink and black oblong beads onto head pins in the following order: bead cup, bead, upside-down bead cup (so it fits like a cap). Now make a loop on the end of the pin. Leave to one side.

4. Thread 2 black and 2 pale pink tubular beads each onto their own eye pins (making 4 in all), trim and make loops at the ends as in step 1. Leave to one side.

step 3   step 4   step 5   step 7

5. Thread 1 dark pink tubular bead, followed by 1 French crimp and 1 black tubular bead, onto an eye pin, finishing off as in step 1. Leave to one side.

6. Repeat step 5.

7. Thread 1 pale pink bead, 1 French crimp, 1 black bead, 1 French crimp and 1 dark pink bead onto an eye pin, and make a loop at the other end.

To join the sections you have constructed onto the jump rings.

8. Hang one of the dark pink oblong beads (step 3) from one of the black tubular beads (step 4). Hang this from the jump ring which links the first two dark pink oblong beads on the necklace front.

9. Repeat step 8 but hang from the jump ring linking the last two dark pink oblong beads on the opposite side of the necklace front.

10. Repeat steps 8 and 9, joining the pale pink tubular beads onto the black oblong beads. Hang from the jump rings between the second and third beads and the sixth and seventh beads on the necklace front.

11. Attach the beads in steps 5 and 6 to the black oblong beads (step 3) and hang from the jump rings between the third and fourth beads and between the fifth and sixth beads on the necklace front.

12. Hang the remaining dark pink oblong bead from the beads from step 7. Hang this from the centre of the necklace front between the fifth and sixth beads.

To finish the necklace.

13. Thread the remaining beads onto pieces of Tiger Tail: start each side with a black bead followed by a pale pink, then a dark pink bead, then back to black, and alternate the remaining beads. Use a French crimp to attach the Tiger Tail to the necklace front.

14. Attach the other ends of the Tiger Tail to the fastening, using French crimps.

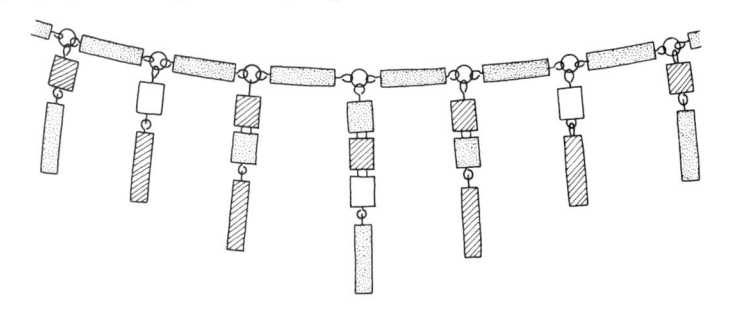

Glass Necklaces

The glass necklaces featured in this book are very different from one another.

1 Marble Necklace

(*see photograph between pages 24–25*)
This necklace is very chunky. The front alternates small glass and marble type beads, which makes the necklace lighter than if just marble beads were used. The back of the necklace is made up of the small paper-filled beads. These are more comfortable than the heavier marble beads and also help the necklace to sit well.

2 Fruit Necklaces

These necklaces are much more delicate than the 'marble' necklace. They are made from glass fruit alternated with faceted glass beads (both from Hobby Horse). The glass beads are there to stop the glass fruits knocking against one another and also for reasons of economy as glass fruit is quite expensive.

The necklace illustrated here is a combination of various fruits using the colours red, mauve, green and aubergine. It is the toning colours which tie the various elements together.

The second necklace (see photograph) is made up of cherries in various sizes, small faceted glass beads and bugles in different shades of red and green. It is a less subtle more 'fun' necklace than the first.

You could also try combinations of bright and exotic fruit to make a 'Carmen Miranda' necklace.

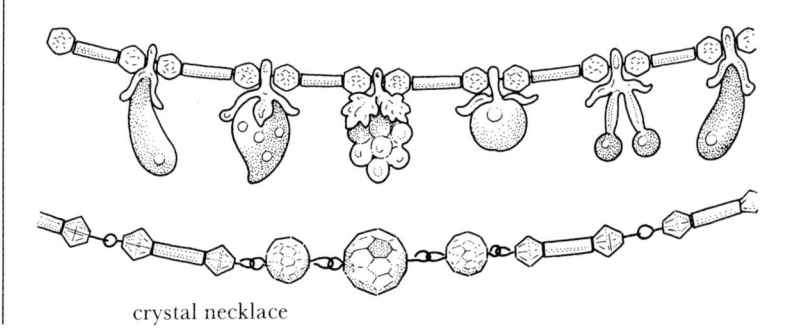

crystal necklace

3 Single Strand Crystal Necklace

A simple one-strand necklace made up of small crystal beads and silver-lined bugles threaded onto silver-coloured eye pins. (Beads from Ells and Farrier, see stockists, page 48).

You could make a pearl chain necklace in the same way as this by replacing the crystal beads with small pearls, threaded onto eye pins and linked together.

1 × 8mm faceted crystal bead
8 × 6mm faceted crystal beads
28 × 3mm faceted crystal beads
14 silver-lined bugle beads
silver eye pins
a jump-ring and a bolt ring

1. Thread a 3mm bead, 1 bugle bead, and another 3mm bead onto an eye pin. Make a loop at the straight end of the eye pin, so that you now have a loop on either end.
2. Repeat step 1 fourteen times. Put the beads to one side.
3. Thread the 8 × 6mm beads each onto their own eye pins, trim the pins and make loops on each as you did for the beads in step 1. Put the beads to one side.
4. Thread the 8mm bead onto an eye pin and make a loop at the end. This will make the centre of the necklace.
5. Join 1 × 6mm bead to either side of this central 8mm bead by linking the loops together.
6. Work from the centre out, doing to one side what you do to the other. On each side join two of the 3mm/bugle/3mm combinations from step 1, then add 1 × 6mm bead.
7. Repeat step 6 twice more on each side, and then finish with 1 × 6mm and a 3mm/bugle/3mm bead combination. Finally, fix the jump ring on one side of the necklace and the bolt ring on the other.

4 Crystal and Pearl Choker

In order for a choker to work it must fit exactly. It is therefore sensible to allow extra thread when making the choker and to work from the middle outwards so that if you have to add or subtract beads you will not spoil the overall design.

The materials given are for a choker measuring 32cm (12½ inches) plus 1cm (½ inch) for the clasp. Allow more beads for a larger neck. The beads may be bought by the string or box from Hobby Horse or The Bead Shop.

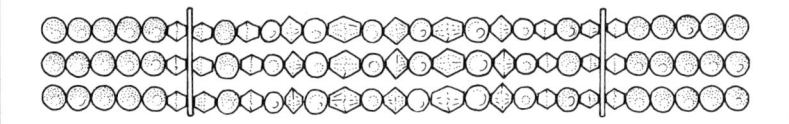

One string or box of each kind will be plenty.

3mm crystal beads
6mm crystal beads
3mm white pearls
4mm white pearls
4mm pink pearls
4mm cream pearls
5mm pink pearls
5mm cream pearls
Tiger Tail
6 crimping beads (French crimps)
4 spacing bars with 3 holes for a 3-strand necklace
a box clasp for a 3-strand necklace

Work from the centre outwards. The directions given are for half a row of beads; the other half of the row is worked in the same way, as are the other two rows. The spacing bars are used to keep the strands of the necklace apart.

1. Thread onto the Tiger Tail the following beads: 1 × 6mm crystal, > 1 × 4mm white pearl, 1 × 6mm crystal, 1 × 5mm cream pearl, 1 × 6mm crystal, 1 × 4mm white pearl, 1 × 3mm crystal, 1 × 5mm pink pearl, 1 × 3mm crystal and then 1 spacing bar through the top hole for the first strand (the middle for the second, the bottom for the third).

2. After the spacing bar, continue threading as follows: 1 × 3mm crystal, 3 × 4mm cream pearls plus 1 × 4mm pink pearl, 3 × 4mm white pearls, 1 × 4mm pink pearl, 3 × 3mm white pearls, 1 × 4mm pink pearl, 1 × 3mm crystal and then another spacing bar.

3. For the final piece, thread on 1 × 3mm crystal, 1 × 4mm pink pearl, 3 × 3mm white pearls, 1 × 4mm pink pearl, 3 × 3mm white pearls, 1 × 4mm pink pearls, 3 × 3mm white pearls, 1 × 3mm crystal. Crimp onto the box clasp.

4. To do the other side of the necklace, work from > in step 1 to the end, remembering that the first 6mm bead you threaded on is the centre of the necklace.

5. Repeat for the other 2 rows.

Other Necklaces

Make necklaces from any of the other 'beads' available from stockists. None are illustrated, but I hope the descriptions will give you inspiration!

Christmas Bauble Necklace
I call it this because the beads, which are covered in thread (silk or synthetic), look exactly like small Christmas tree decorations. They come in very bright colours – I've used green, red, yellow and purple together – and I finish off with 2 gold beads and a gold fastening at the back.

Metallic Bead Necklace
This is a rather military looking necklace, with its large gold beads of varying sizes and shapes in copper and brass coloured metals.

Clear Plastic Bead Necklace
Very chunky white plastic beads are alternated with elongated plastic beads of a translucent pale blue colour. They are threaded onto leather thonging and knotted between beads. Simple but effective.

'Ivory' Necklace
'Ivory' plastic beads are available from Hobby Horse. The necklace is made up from large oval beads, round beads which look as though they have been flattened, and with 2 or 3 washers threaded between each bead. The result is a fairly classic necklace which could be worn on most occasions.

Bead Earrings

Traditionally earrings have been worn in pairs, except by pirates who are generally pictured wearing a hoop in one ear. Sailors used to wear gold earrings so that, wherever they were, they carried the price of a decent burial on their bodies! Gypsies wear an earring in one ear or the other to indicate their married state.

Homosexuals used to wear an earring in the left ear if they were passive and in the right ear if they were active. However, since ear-piercing has become widespread throughout the heterosexual, as well as homosexual, community, this is no longer applicable.

In the Asian community ear piercing was done as a cure for short sightedness.

Today people often have their ears pierced in several places on the lobe. They may wear one earring alone or an odd assortment. As with other forms of dress, it is a matter of personal taste. If you don't have pierced ears there are different kinds of findings for non-pierced ears.

As earring findings are small and easily lost, I find it convenient to store them in an ice-cube tray.

Basic Hanging Earring

1 head pin
a bead cup
enough beads to fit on the head pin
a clip-on ear finding with a loop or a kidney wire
round-nosed jewellers' pliers

1. Thread the bead cup onto the head pin, so that it looks like a saucer.
2. Thread on the beads, leaving 5mm (¼ inch) of wire showing. Trim off any excess.
3. Grasp the spare wire with the round-nosed pliers and bend it into a loop so that it touches the shaft of the pin (fig 1).
4. Adjust the loop with the pliers so that the wire hangs from the centre of the loop.
5. Attach the loop to the bump in the kidney wire, or to the loop of the ear clip (fig 2).
6. Close all the loops with the round nose pliers.

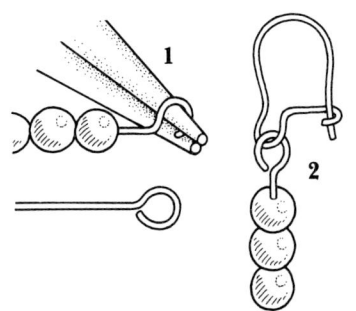

VARIATIONS

1. Use an eye pin instead of a head pin and hang beads from the eye.
2. Hang 2 or 3 pins from one earring finding. The most successful way of doing this is to cut the pins to different lengths, hang these from a jump ring and attach the jump ring to the finding. I've done this on a multi-strand earring with moons, shell, glass and pearl

—36—

beads (see photograph opposite page 24).

3. Make an earring using an eye pin and then hang a large shaped bead from a bail. The photograph opposite page 24 shows mother of pearl beads and a star, but I've also done this with a faceted plastic bead with a large plastic heart hanging from it, and bluey-green plastic heart beads and a star.

4. Use a spacer bar – an attractive patterned piece of wire – rather than a pin for a more decorative effect.

5. Many earrings can be made by simply joining a bead, shell or interesting shape onto a finding. Ideas include: shell, spun-glass hoops, carved leaf, spun glass spirals, green glass pendants, plastic pendants, painted wooden beads, little bottles, jokes and toys – the possibilites are infinite! See some examples in the photograph opposite page 24.

Spiral Earring

blue glass silver paper lined beads
yellow and orange striped beads
6mm wire
1 head pin
1 ear clip or *kidney wire*

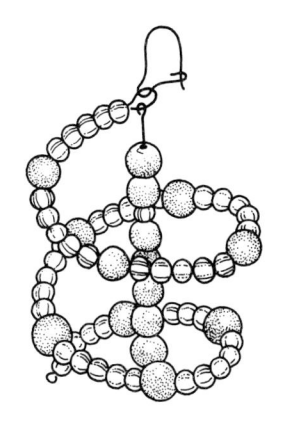

1. Cut a strip of wire approximately 23cm (9 inches) long.
2. Bend the wire round a small cylinder such as a pot of herbs, or small jar of paint, so that it forms a spiral.
3. Make a small loop at one end of the spiral and then thread on the beads. I used 5 yellow and orange striped ones, with every sixth bead being a blue paper filled one (The Bead Shop).
4. Make a loop at the other end of the spiral and then hang it from the kidney wire or ear clip.
5. Thread beads onto the eye pin. I used blue with a yellow and orange striped one near the top.

Hang the eye pin from the kidney wire or earclip, so that it hangs down the centre of the spiral.

Flower Earrings

Many bead shops such as Hobby Horse sell plaster flowers. These may be put together with beads and pins to create flower earrings.

The materials given are for one earring only: double the quantities for a pair.

Flower Earring 1
This earring is reminiscent of a freesia with its brightly coloured top and dangling centre.

2 × 6mm crystal beads
3 × 3mm crystal beads
1 eye pin
3 head pins
1 pink 3-pronged plaster flower shape
1 ear hook with a loop

1. Thread 1 × 6mm bead, the flower shape and the other 6mm bead onto the eye pin.
2. Make a loop at the other end of the eye pin and attach it to the loop of the ear hook.
3. Cut the head pins into different lengths.
4. Thread a 3mm bead on to each head pin.
5. Make a loop at the end of each head pin and attach to the loop which is under the flower shape.

Flower Earring 2
This earring looks like a daisy and is very simple to make. It can be varied by using a 3-pronged shape as in the earring above and sticking that into the centre of the daisy shape, followed by the bead. Use different colours for maximum effect.

1 plaster daisy shape in blue
1 white bead to fit in the centre of the daisy
1 clip-on earring base
impact adhesive

1. Stand the daisy in something to stop it wobbling about – a piece of plasticine perhaps.
2. Stick the bead into the daisy centre with the adhesive.
3. Turn the daisy upside down and glue the earring base on to the underside of the daisy.

Flower Earring 3

This earring is made using a bell-shaped plaster flower in red. See photograph opposite page 24.

1 red bell-shaped plaster flower
1 bell cap (gold coloured)
impact adhesive
2 small red beads
1 bead cup (gold coloured)
3 head pins (gold coloured)
1 earring finding with a loop

1. Thread the bead cup onto a head pin and push it from the top through the flower so that the pin sticks out at the bottom.
2. Glue the cup into place, on top of the flower.
3. Make a loop at the end of the head pin.
4. Stick the bell cap over the pin and bead cup at the top fo the flower.
5. Thread the 2 small beads onto the remaining 2 head pins (make them different lengths).
6. Attach the pins to the loop in the flower centre.
7. Attach the flower to the earring loop.

Hoop Earrings

You can buy ready-made hoops, or make your own from 6mm or 8mm wire. To make the loop bend the wire round a small cylinder. You could also suspend rings – curtain rings even – from findings. See opposite page 24 for several examples.

Hoop Earring 1

This earring is made up from sequins – which you can buy in a multitude of colours. They look wonderfully effective en masse like this.

12cm (about 5 inches) wire
sequins
kidney hook
1 jump ring

1. Bend the wire round a small cylinder.
2. Thread on the sequins to within 5mm (¼ inch) of each end of the wire. Straighten the last 5mm (¼ inch) of wire.
3. Make 2 loops with the straightened ends of the wire by bending them around the round-nosed pliers.
4. Attach to the jump ring.
5. Join the jump ring onto the kidney hook.

Hoop Earring 2

A pretty hoop earring using glass leaves, flowers, bugles and rocaille beads, with hanging head pins of bugles and rocailles.

12cm (about 5 inches) wire
3 head pins
glass rocailles
glass bugles
glass leaves and flowers
1 jump ring

1. Cut and bend the wire as in loop earring 1.
2. Thread on glass bugles, flowers and leaves.
3. Attach the loops to the jump ring.
4. Thread the remaining beads onto the head pins, make loops in their ends and attach to jump ring.
5. Attach the jump ring to the kidney hoop.

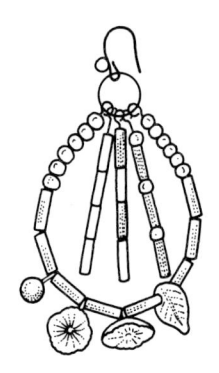

Other Earrings

Large Crystal Earrings with Bows

These are very heavy earrings indeed – not for all-day wear!

1 large crystal glass drop (available Ells and Farrier).
1 large faceted glass bead
1 bail
1 earring clip or wire with a loop
1 eye pin
enough 6mm (¼ inch) ribbon to make a bow. (Allow more than you need as they are very fiddly to tie!)

1. Attach the bail to the crystal drop.
2. Attach the bail to the eye pin.
3. Leaving a gap on which to tie a bow, make a loop on the other end of the eye pin and attach it to the bail.
4. Tie the bow onto the pin so that the bead is above it and the drop below.
5. Attach to the hook on the earring finding.

Red Oblong Diamanté Earring

This is a stud earring instead of a drop one, made with red faceted diamanté which is mounted. You simply have to stick a pierced earring finding with a stud (to stick) and stick it onto the back of the diamanté mount with impact adhesive (see photograph opposite page 24).

A very simple idea which you can adapt to many other mounts or flat-bottomed beads.

Non-pierced ear findings can be used too.

Coin Earring

(*see photograph opposite page 24*)

3 coin shapes with holes in the tops (Ells and Farrier)
3 gold-coloured eye pins
a few gold and amber coloured bugles and rocailles
gold jump ring and kidney wire

1. Cut the eye pins into 3 different lengths.
2. Thread the rocailles and bugle beads onto the eye pins.
3. Attach the pins to the jump ring and the ring to the kidney wire.
4. Attach the coins onto the eyes of the eye pins.

Make similar earrings using combinations of drop-shaped stones, plastic and diamanté, and textured metal beads.

Bead Hair Decoration

Before starting to make hair decorations look in the costume departments of museums. The Victoria and Albert Museum in London has some excellent examples of hair combs and tiaras.

Books on Art Nouveau jewellery are especially useful, as are books on the history of costume. The work of Erté, the artist and designer, contains fine examples of hair decoration.

Try looking around antique shops and auctions. It is still possible to pick up beaded caps of the 1920s and other attractive period pieces.

Decorating a Hair Comb

One way of decorating a hair comb is to sew beads onto it. The easiest way to do this is to cover the top of the comb with a stretchy fine meshed fabric onto which beads may be sewn.

The material most suitable for this purpose is corset elastic. It is available from most haberdashery departments and comes in black, flesh or white. If you cannot find this, use either netting or ordinary elastic, or a stretch fabric such as jersey.

Another way of decorating a hair comb is to thread beads onto thin wire and arrange them in a pattern at the front of the comb: use blue rocailles and bugles on a red comb, for instance. You can also simply glue mounted diamantés onto the front of the comb.

Hair Comb

hair comb
corset elastic
a few each of the following: rocaille beads, bugles, translucent plastic or glass butterflies, flowers or leaves

1. Cut a piece of elastic fabric twice the height of the top of the comb.

2. Cover the top of the comb with the elasticated fabric and sew into place through the prongs, joining both sides neatly together.

3. Sew bugle beads, rocailles and small glass butterflies and flowers onto the comb top until all the elastic is covered. It's a fairly long and intricate task, but the result is worth it.

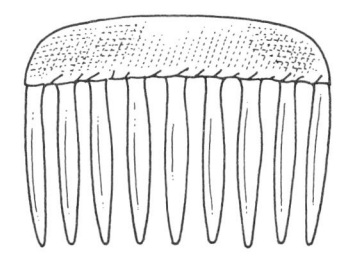

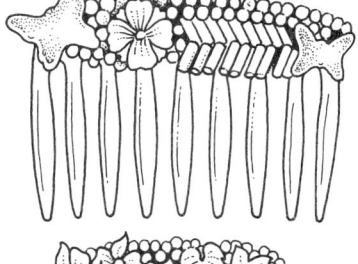

4. You could also hang leaves and flowers off the comb on strands of embroidery silk so that they hang down in the hair. Or hang fine feathers and bugle beads similarly.

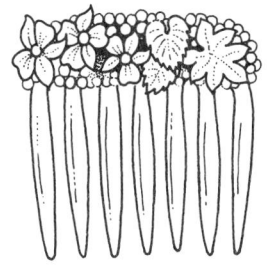

Sewing with Beads

It was the Egyptians who first developed the art of bead embroidery, using it to decorate their garments and also their mummies. Beads were used extensively in Victorian and Edwardian costume, including the decoration of buttons, bags, collars and other accessories. The flappers of the 1920s had their dresses encrusted with rocailles and bugles. These dresses can still be bought in antique shops or picked up at auctions. Examples of old beadwork can be seen in the photograph opposite page 25.

After the austerity years of World War II, there was a renewal of interest in bead work which resulted in flamboyant creations on the couture evening gowns of the early 1950s. Later that decade, lambswool sweaters and cardigans with elaborate patterns of bead work became very fashionable. Many of these can still be found. The garments were lined in silk to help take the weight of the beads and to stop the wool stretching.

In the last few years, with the move towards more glamorous evening wear, there has been a revival of interest in beaded clothes, and it's a huge economy to be able to think of doing it yourself.

When applying beads to a garment, an attractive effect may often be achieved by decorating only a small section of the garment. For example, enhance a little black dress with a collar of silver bugle beads or diamanté straps. Diamanté may be bought in strip form from Ells and Farrier.

Beaded motifs may be bought ready made in good haberdashery departments. To decorate a garment, you just sew on the motif.

One way of applying beads to woollen garments is to make them part of an appliquéd motif which is worked as a complete unit and then sewn onto the garment in its finished state. This stops the wool pulling and is easy to remove for washing.

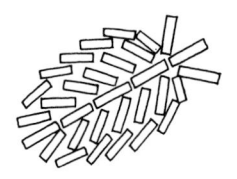

Another idea for loose-knit woollens is to weave beads in and out across the rows.

1. Thread wool onto a darning or embroidery needle and make a knot in the end.

2. Bring the needle up from the wrong side of the garment to the top and thread on a bead.

3. Make a stitch, thus anchoring the bead in position, and take the needle back to the wrong side of the garment.

4. Repeat steps 2 and 3 until you reach the end of the row, then finish off with a few stitches on the wrong side of the knitting.

5. Work other rows the same way.

Small pearls or rocailles can be sewn onto fine-knit sweaters.

Designing

Decide what it is you wish to achieve. Do you wish to draw attention to a certain part of the body? Are you trying to liven up a boring dress? Have you nothing special to wear for a party? Do you just wish to make something totally original?

Here are a few suggestions.

1. Before you start any sewing, place the beads next to each other and try out different combinations of beads for size and colour.
2. Emphasise the shoulders on an old sweater by inserting shoulder pads, and sewing metallic beads onto the shoulders to look like epaulettes.
3. Make a 'sky at night' sweater by sewing on random stars and moon beads.
4. Watch television programmes like *Dallas* and *Dynasty* to see where those little touches of beadwork go on a cocktail dress!
5. If you have a slim waist, emphasise it by making a beaded belt to wear with a plain evening dress.
6. Look at the work of well-known designers. Kriza makes wonderful animal appliqués. You could do something similar with beads.
7. Sew a few delicate beads onto a piece of beautiful silk underwear.
8. Dandify a waistcoat with bead decoration.
9. Make a party top. Sew beads onto net, then sew the net onto a plain T-shirt or camisole. Cut the backing away where the netting lies.

Bead Weaving

Bead weaving is very easy and one can produce incredible results without buying expensive equipment. It is a means of producing strips of beads easily. These can be used as necklaces or sewn onto belts, bangles or clothes.

Before starting your piece of weaving, look at traditional Indian motifs for design inspiration – most American Indian beadwork was traditionally made by this method. These designs will look best made up in bright opaque rocaille beads. Another source of inspiration is the beaded dresses of the 1920s. These were made up in glass bugles, rocailles and sequins. And again, before starting, read the following details and then draw your design on graph paper with one square being equal to one bead.

Weaving beads is similar to weaving cloth in that there are warp threads (running from top to bottom) which are held in tension on the loom, and a weft thread (this goes across) which carries the beads. The weft thread is woven in and out of the warp thread.

Bead looms can be bought from Hobby Horse and other good craft shops. They come with a spring at each end, to separate the warp thread, and rollers to wind on the work. They have full threading instructions.

Make your own bead loom by using the base of a strong cardboard box. Notch at intervals of 2mm (about ⅛–⅒ inch). Wind the thread – as tightly as you can – round the box and through the notches (fig 1). Or make a wooden loom and attach the threads onto tacks (fig 2).

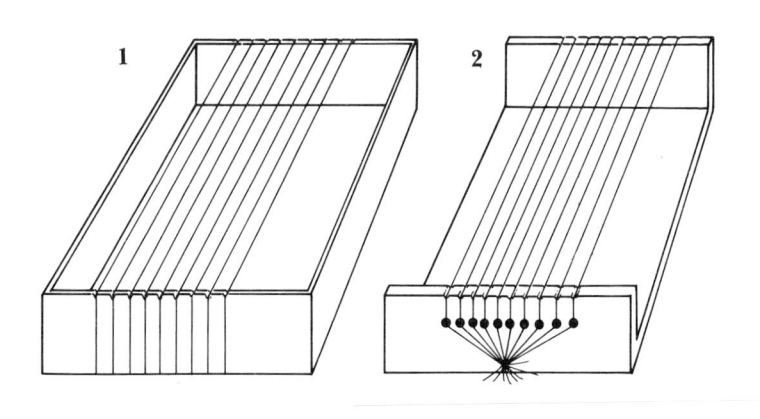

The best thread to use is a buttonhole thread as this is very strong. You need one thread more than the number of beads in the width of the design: for 6 beads use 7 warp threads.

Weaving

rocaille beads (quantity depends on what you are weaving)
beading needle (a long, very fine needle)
bead loom
beading thread

1. Thread the loom (see above).
2. Cut another piece of thread as long as you can easily manage without it getting in a knot.
3. Thread one end of this onto a beading needle and tie the other end onto the first warp thread at the beginning. This is now the weft thread.
4. Put the correct number of beads (the same number of beads as there are gaps between threads) onto the weft thread.
5. Pass the needle and beads underneath the warp threads, and position the beads so that each bead is in a gap between the threads.

6. With a finger underneath, push the beads up so their tops are just above the warp threads. Pass the needle and weft thread back through the beads over the warp threads. This will secure the beads in place (fig 3).

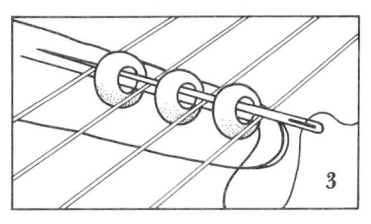

7. Continue working from one side to the other.
8. When you have finished, weave the weft thread back into the last line of beads.
9. Cut off the warp threads, leaving enough ends to tie together or to sew between the beadwork and any material that you are backing it with.

Acknowledgements

Many thanks to the following:

Sally Lang for helping check proofs.

Wendy Butters for help in making samples.

Mickey from Hobby Horse for her time and help.

Hobby Horse for their generosity in supplying me with beads, findings, and threads.

Ells and Farrier Ltd for their generosity in supplying me with beads, sequins, diamanté, and findings.

The Bead Shop for their generosity in supplying me with beads and findings.

Dave Solsbury for his advice.

Fulham Pottery for their generosity in supplying me with cold clay.

Stockists

Hobby Horse
15–17 Langton Street, London SW10, and 11 Blue Boar Street, Oxford.
Hobby Horse runs a wholesale mail-order service.

The Bead Shop
43 Neal Street, London WC2H 9PJ.
The Bead Shop runs a mail-order service for wholesale and retail customers.

Ells and Farrier Ltd
5 Princes Street, Hanover Square, London W1.
Mail-order service from: Unit 26, Chiltern Trading Estate, Earl Howe Road, Holmer Green, High Wycombe, Buckinghamshire.

The Fulham Pottery Ltd
184 New Kings Road, London SW6 4PB.